Spells for the Afterlife

The Book of the Dead

Ancient Egypt History Facts Books
Children's Ancient History

Speedy Publishing LLC
40 E. Main St. #1156
Newark, DE 19711
www.speedypublishing.com

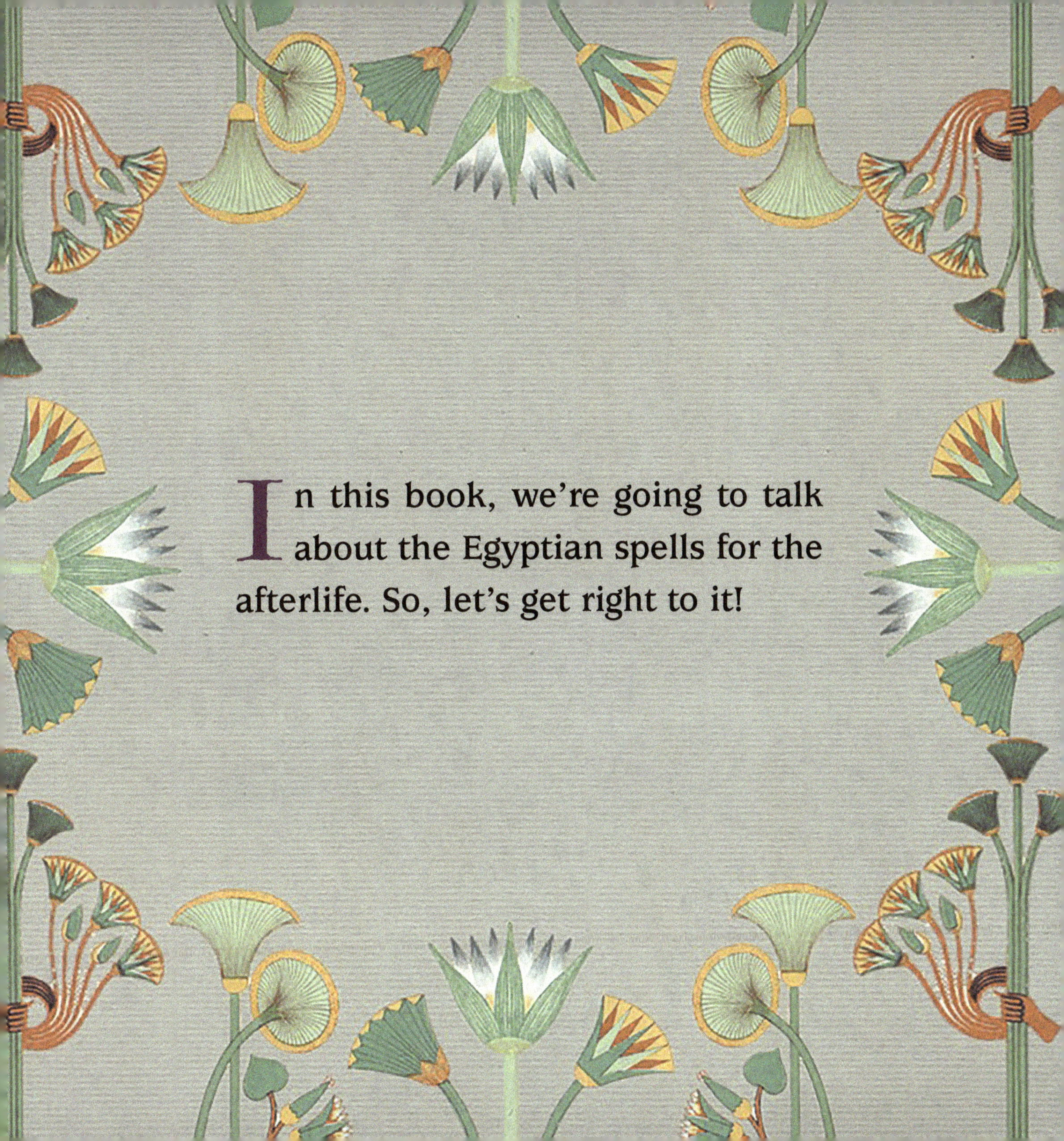

In this book, we're going to talk about the Egyptian spells for the afterlife. So, let's get right to it!

The Ancient Egyptians believed strongly in the afterlife. They prepared the dead person for his or her next life by performing a number of rituals. They mummified the person's body in readiness for their judgment.

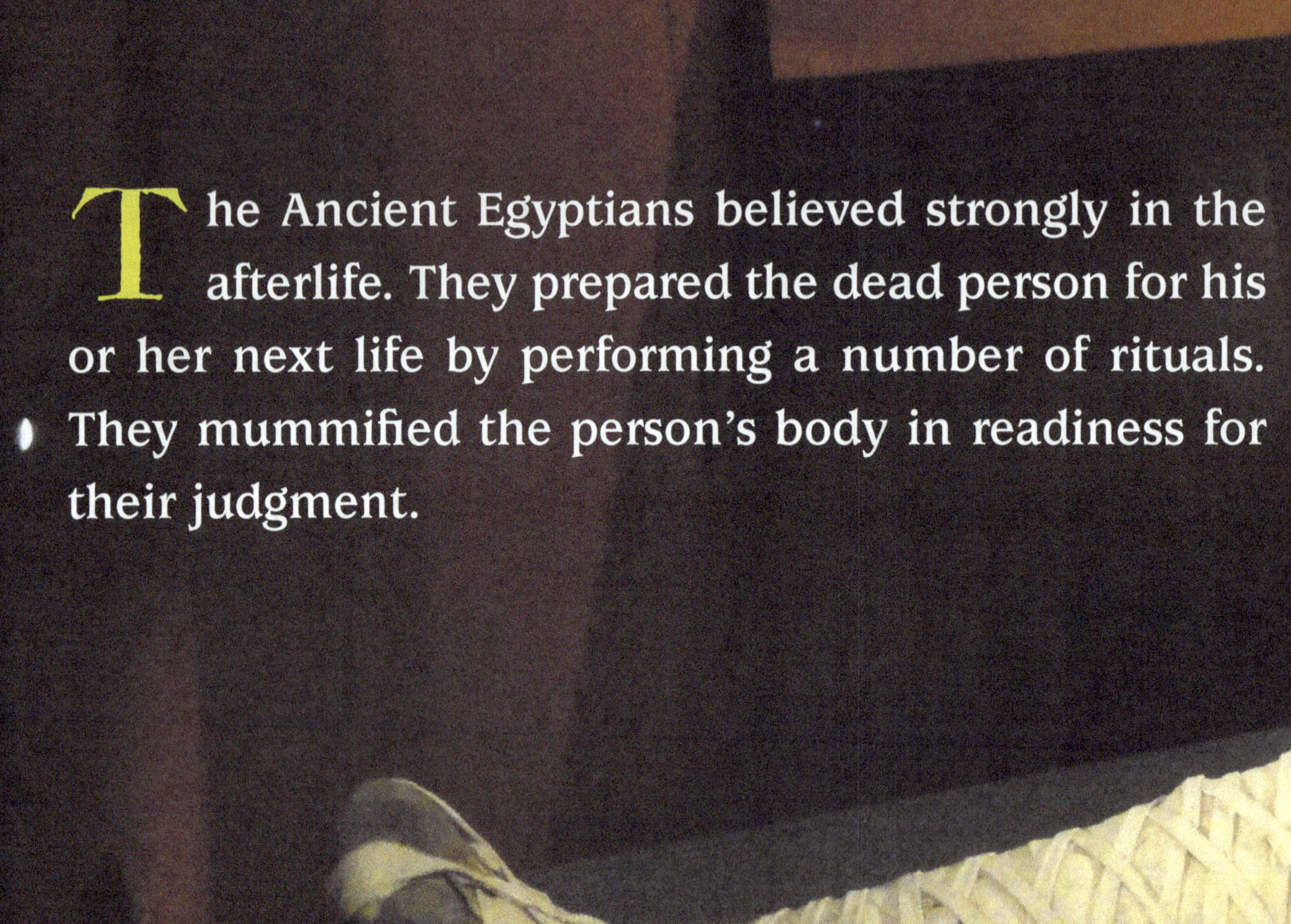

They also placed the person's possessions in the tomb so these objects could be used in the next life. Models of workers were placed in the tomb so the deceased person would have help performing tasks.

In addition to this, in many tombs, there was a special book. This book was either written on sheets of papyrus, an ancient type of paper, or written directly on the tomb's walls. Each book in every tomb was slightly different.

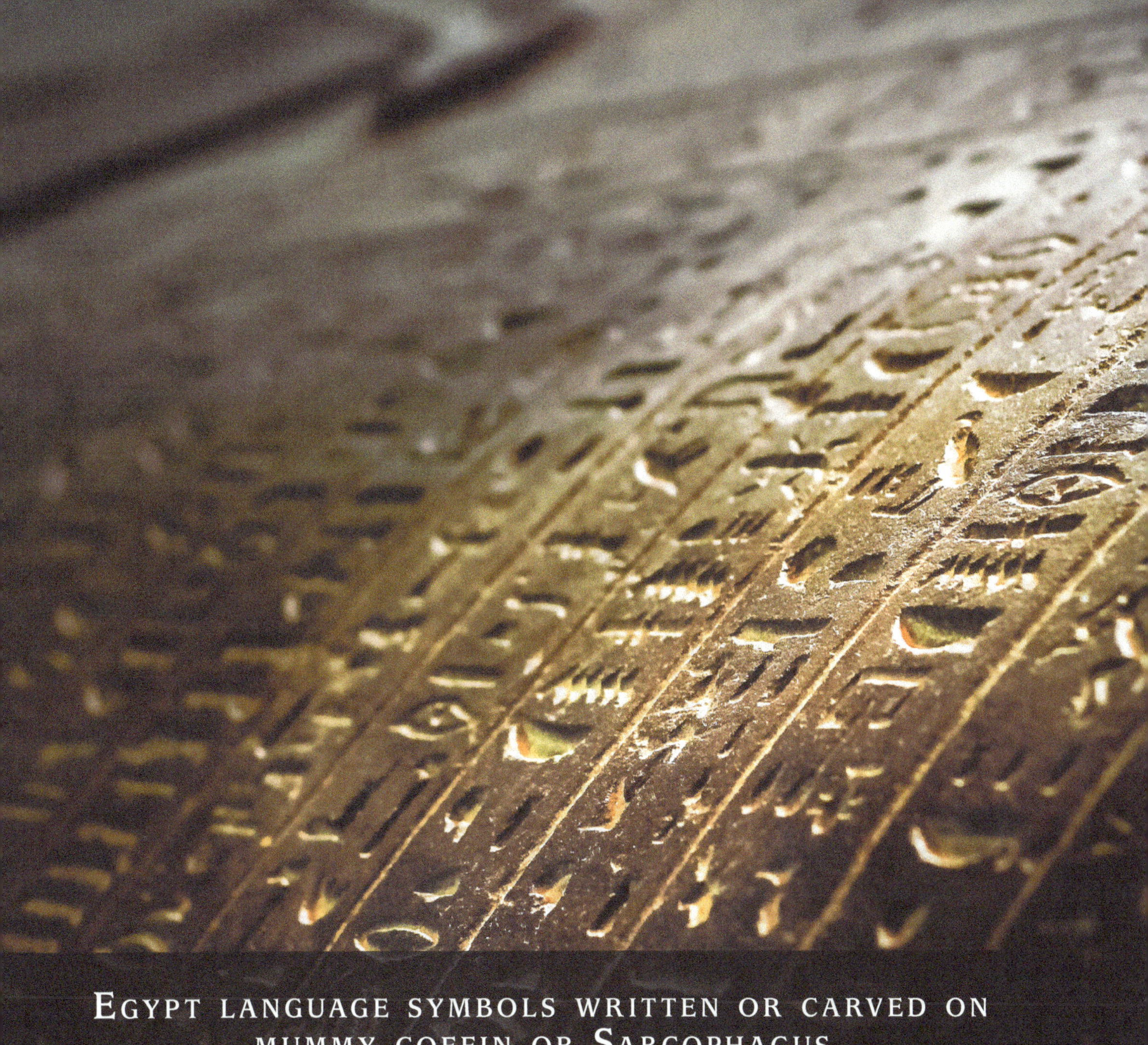

Egypt language symbols written or carved on mummy coffin or Sarcophagus

Egyptian painting

It was customized for the individual's life. In addition to the text in the book, there were very colorful illustrations showing the different beings that the dead person would encounter and depicting the future events.

The Egyptian title for this book translated to something like "spells for coming forth into the day." However, when archaeologists and scholars

from the west first saw the books and decoded the Egyptian hieroglyphics they translated it to "The Book of the Dead."

WHAT WAS INSIDE THE BOOK OF THE DEAD?

The Book of the Dead was essentially a guidebook. It consisted of a series of spells to help the person who was taking the journey into the next life. After all, the afterlife was a lot different than life on Earth.

Detail of ancient Book of the Dead

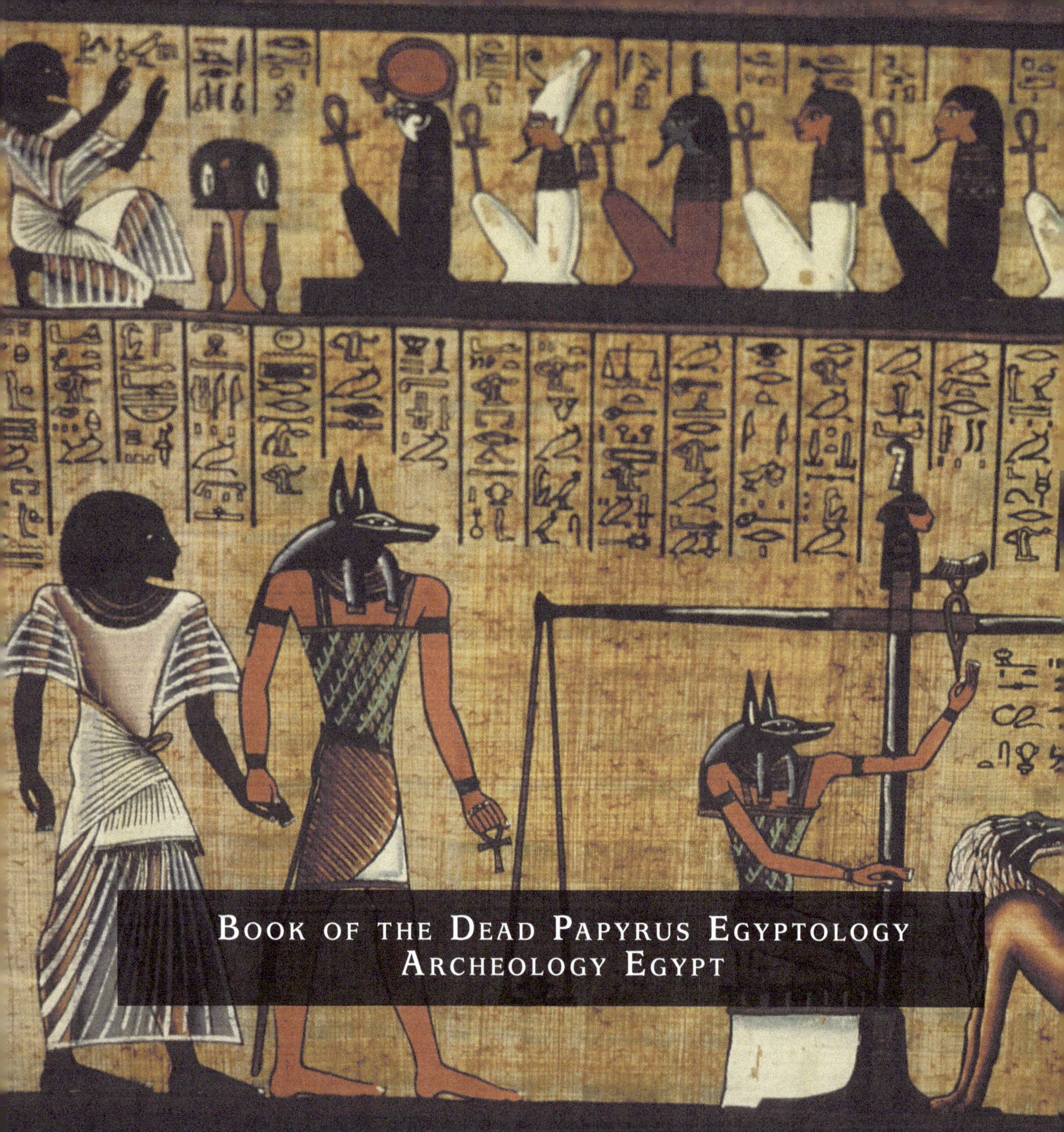
Book of the Dead Papyrus Egyptology
Archeology Egypt

If the deceased person had a guidebook to help, he or she could navigate the new life experiences much more easily. In those days, putting together a book was a very difficult and expensive process since all the text as well as the illustrations had to be created by scribes who had mastered both text and art.

Only the wealthy could afford the most elaborate customized versions of The Book of the Dead. The important Pharaohs and the wealthy elite had books with special spells that had been created just for them.

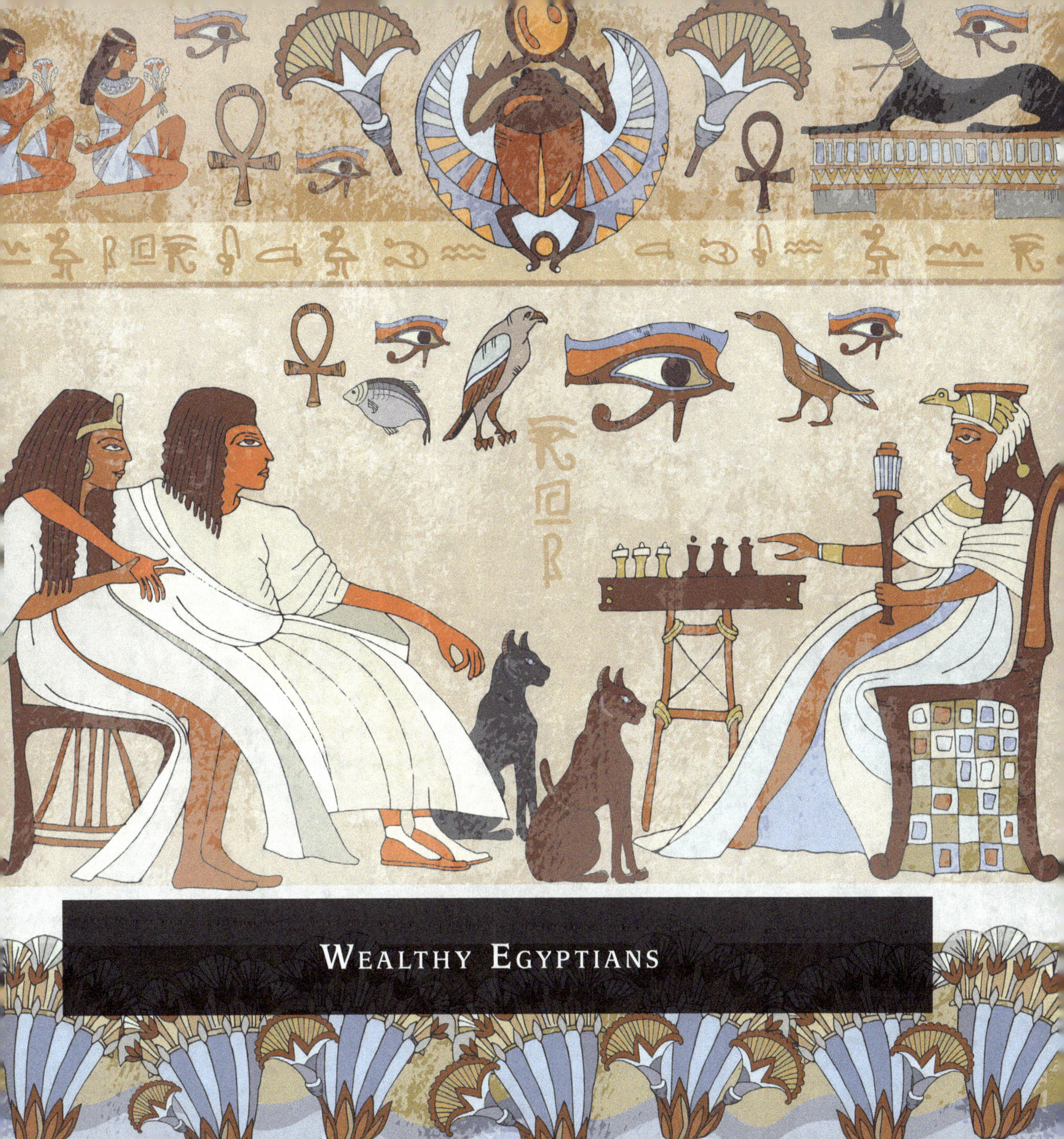

Wealthy Egyptians

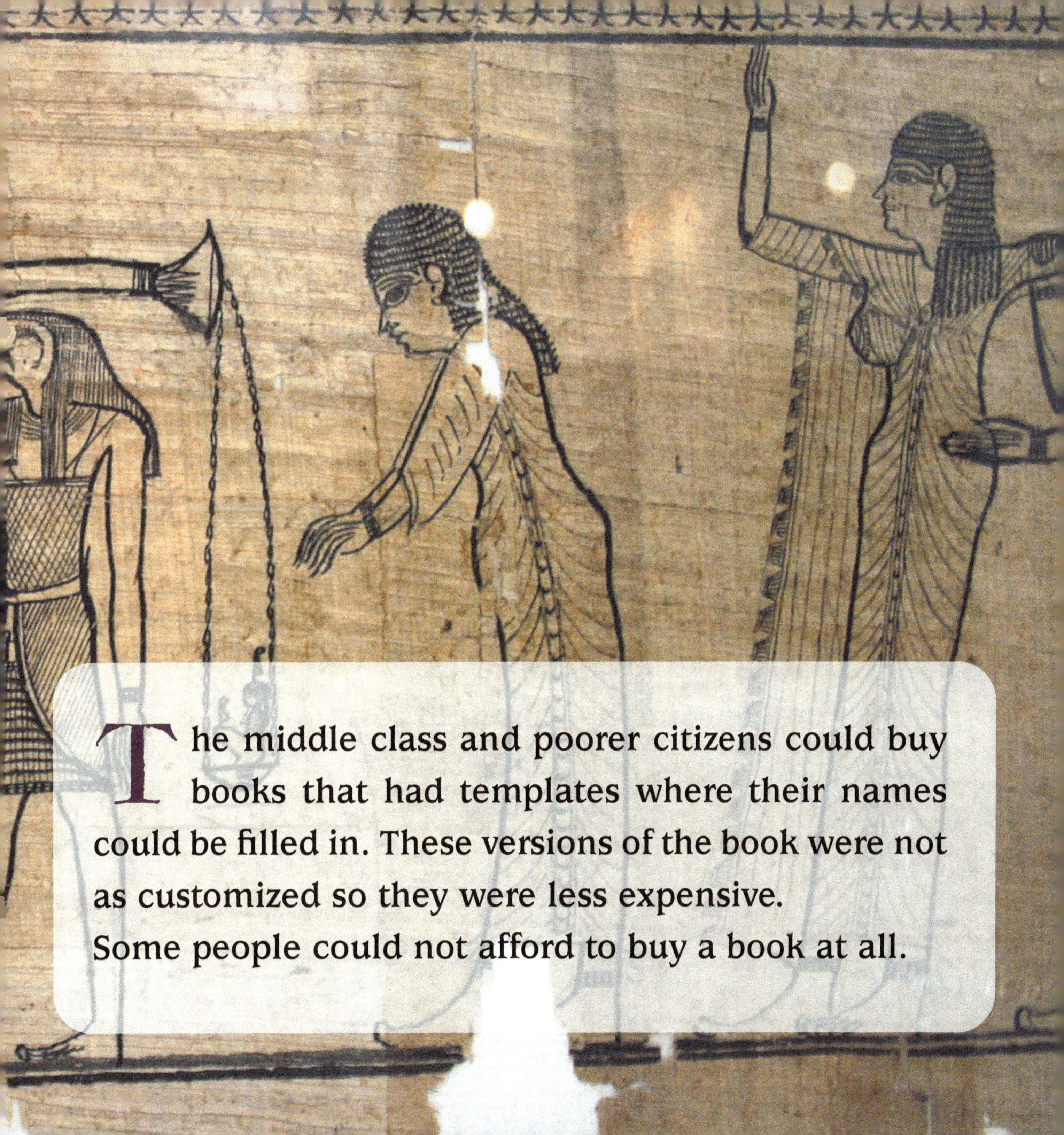

The middle class and poorer citizens could buy books that had templates where their names could be filled in. These versions of the book were not as customized so they were less expensive.

Some people could not afford to buy a book at all.

The book wasn't a running text or story. Instead, it was a collection of chants, spells, magical prayers, and spiritual rituals designed to help the dead person in the afterlife. The spells were designed to offer them protection from the demons in the underworld and give them the power to travel and continue their life in a different form.

The Egyptian civilization thrived for over 3,000 years so The Book of the Dead evolved during that time and different versions were created. Certain gods and goddesses went in and out of favor and this was reflected in the different versions. Historians believe that the stories were from varying traditions because the wording is different in different parts of the book.

HOW OLD IS THE BOOK OF THE DEAD?

The original spells for The Book of the Dead were first put down into text form around 1600 BC. It's more than likely that the original spells existed for many years prior to this and were transmitted in oral storytelling before they were written.

FRAGMENT OF A COFFIN WITH TEXTS FROM THE BOOK OF DEAD

HOW MANY CHAPTERS DID THE BOOK OF THE DEAD CONTAIN?

The Book of the Dead contained over 190 chapters. The earliest versions of the book were just a series of spells loosely organized together. However, later versions of the book were organized into sections based on the process of the journey within the afterlife.

The processes of the deceased going into the tomb and then entering the underworld were described within the first 16 chapters. Then, the guidebook went on to explain which gods could protect and assist the deceased person in his or her new life. The next section outlined the travels and journeys that the deceased person would take. The last section told how the person could come into power in the afterlife as he or she had on Earth.

Opening of the mouth Ceremony

ORISIS
GOD OF THE DEAD

THE WEIGHING OF THE HEART RITUAL

One of the most important spells in the book discusses the judgment of a person's heart. The god of the underworld, Osiris, and a group including over 40 other gods and goddesses were involved in deciding whether a dead person was worthy to move to the afterlife or if he or she would die forever, never to return.

The deceased person had to go through a process to declare that he or she hadn't committed a long list of offenses.

This process of "confessing" that the offenses hadn't been committed was called the "negative confession."

The spirit of the deceased person had to enter a place called "The Hall of Two Truths." The two truths were good and evil. The god Thoth, who was the scribe of the other gods, took the notes about the confession to be recorded. The written account of the judgment process was accompanied by an image of the person's heart on the tray of a scale.

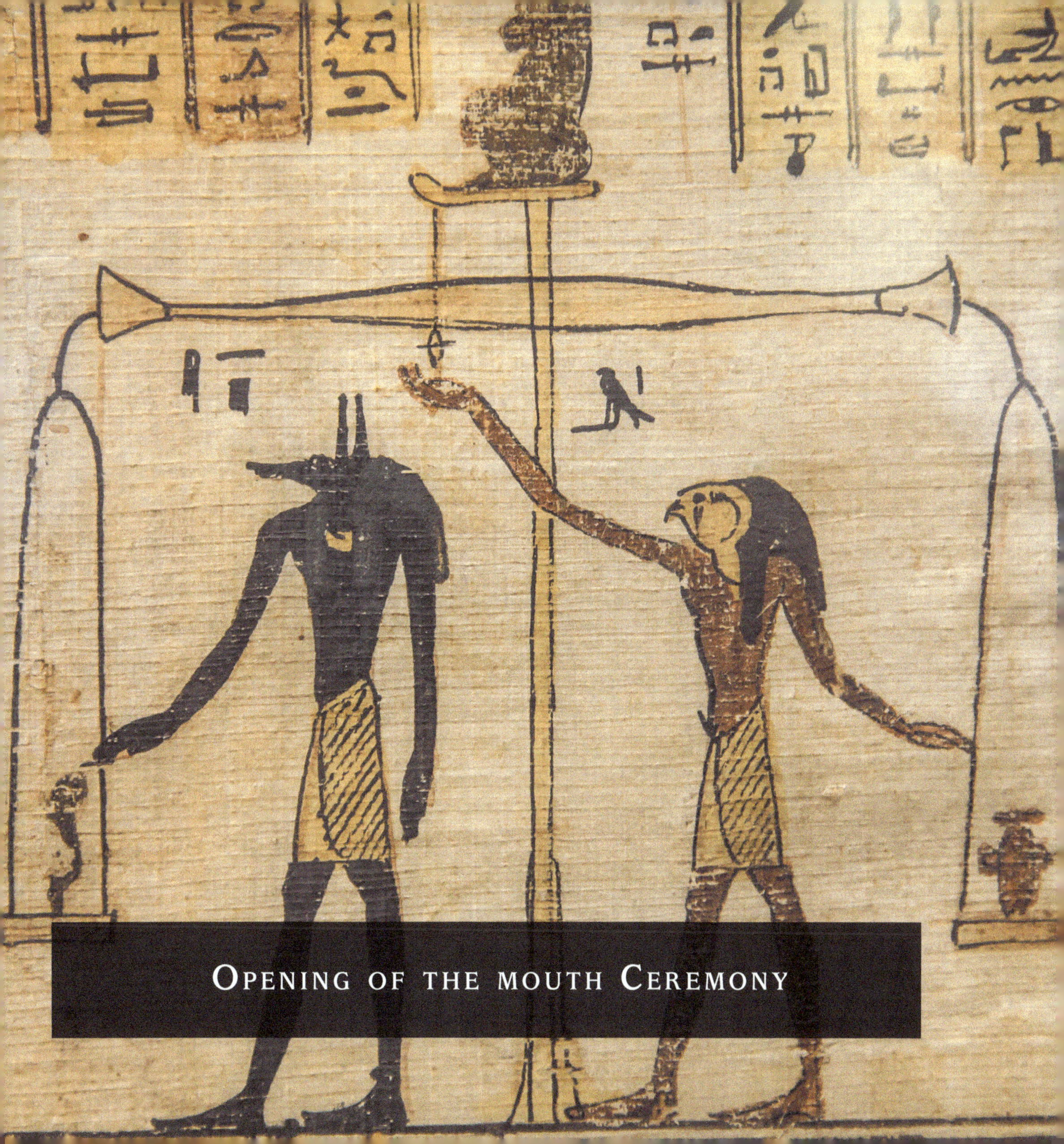

OPENING OF THE MOUTH CEREMONY

Ammat

If the heart balanced against the feather of Ma'at, the goddess of truth, then the person was "light-hearted" and could enter the afterlife. However, if the person had a heavy heart, he or she was refused entrance to the afterlife. The horrible demon Ammat would consume the heart. Ammat was a combination of the head of a crocodile, the body and front legs of a big cat, and the back legs of a hippo.

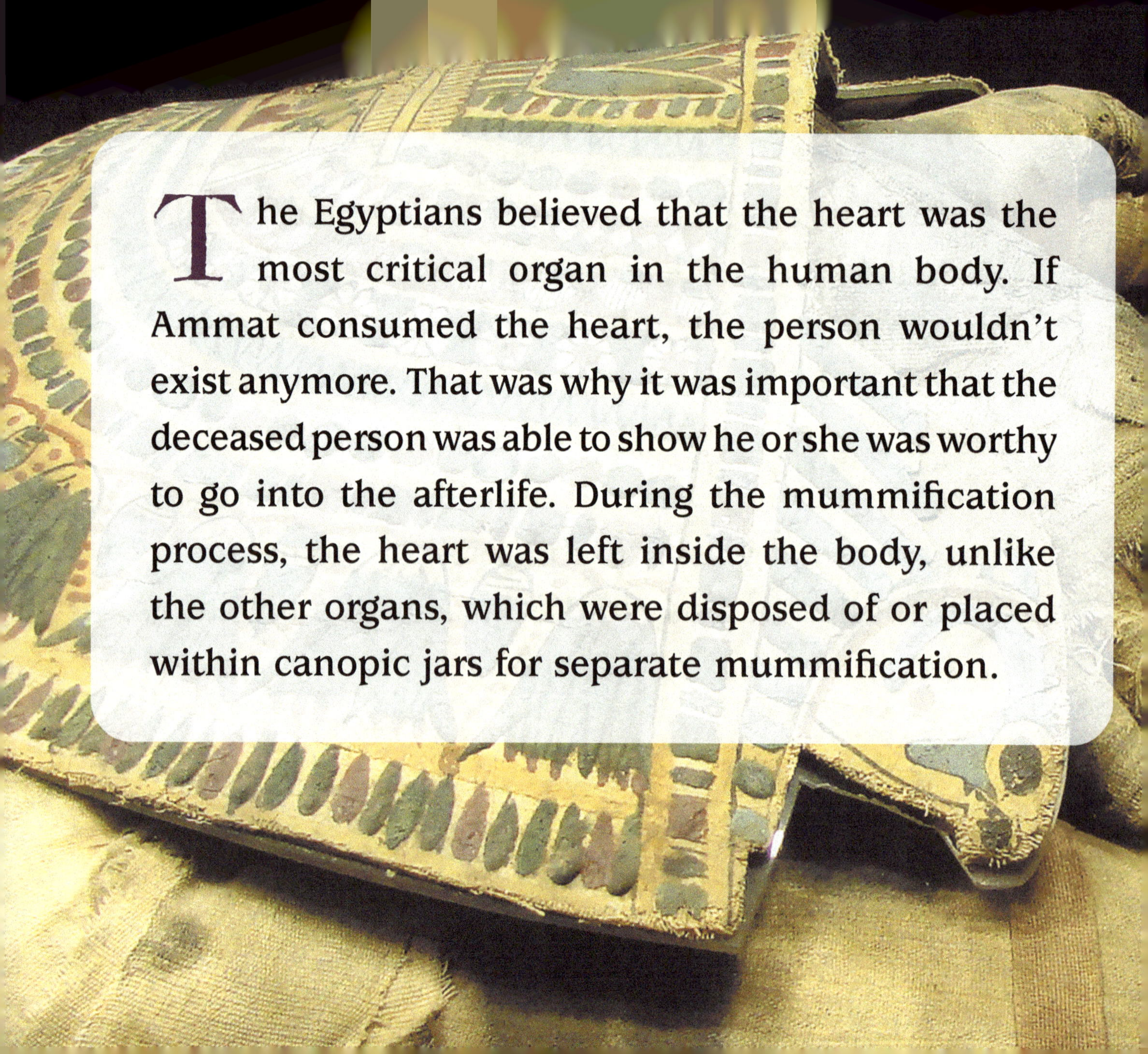

The Egyptians believed that the heart was the most critical organ in the human body. If Ammat consumed the heart, the person wouldn't exist anymore. That was why it was important that the deceased person was able to show he or she was worthy to go into the afterlife. During the mummification process, the heart was left inside the body, unlike the other organs, which were disposed of or placed within canopic jars for separate mummification.

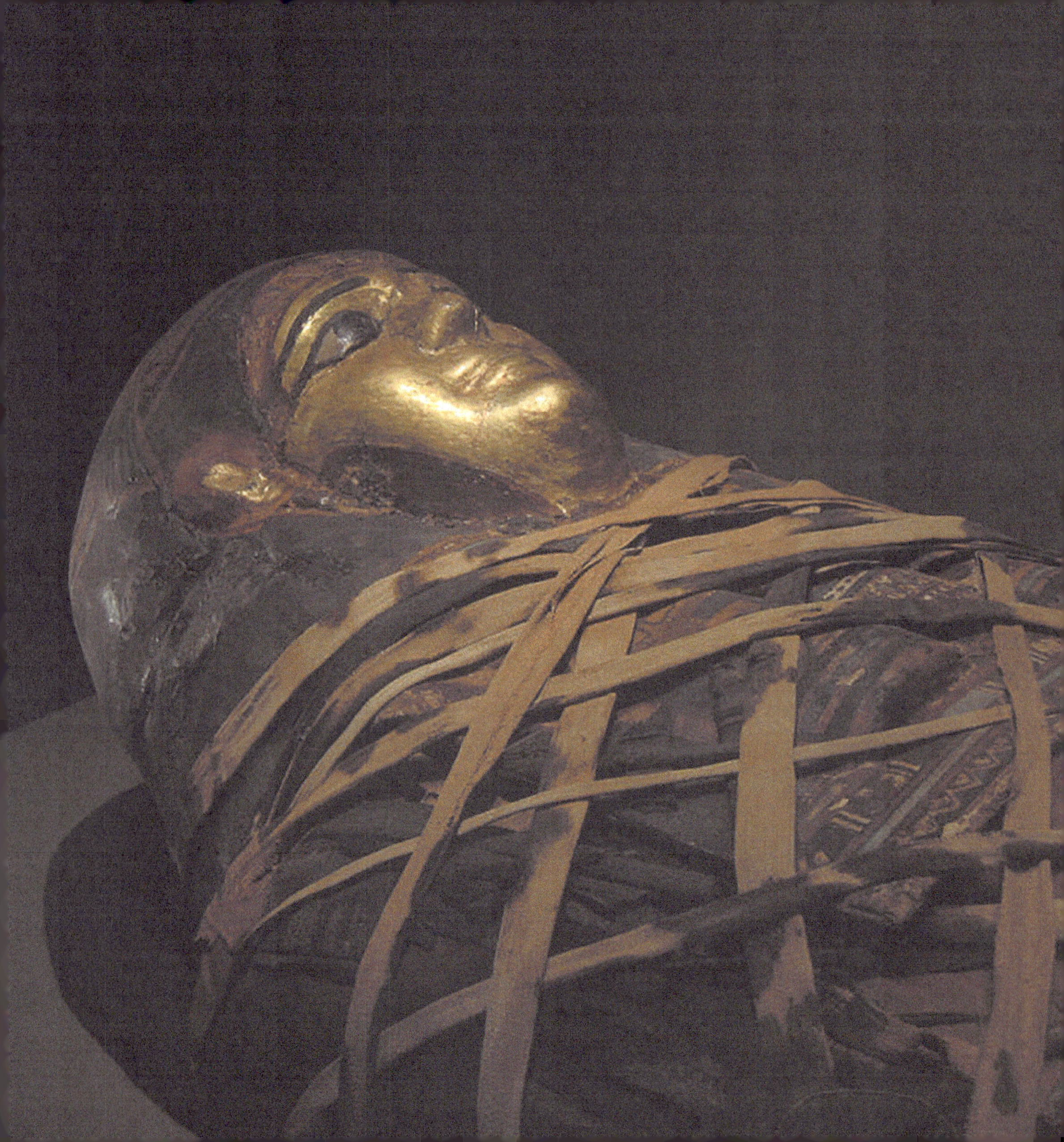

THE FOUR SECTIONS OF THE BOOK OF THE DEAD

The Book of the Dead provides a roadmap of what will happen to a person after she or he passes away.

SECTION 1: CHAPTERS 1 TO 16

The deceased goes into his or her prepared tomb as a mummy. The soul then journeys to the Tuat, which is the underworld. At this point, the soul reunites with the mummified body. The person can now move and speak once more.

SECTION 2: CHAPTERS 17 TO 63

Once the deceased person has been deemed worthy, he or she takes a blessed trip on the boat belonging to the powerful sun god named Ra. The soul's journey to Tuat includes a special meeting with the god of the underworld called Osiris.

SECTION 4: CHAPTERS 130-189

Those who are worthy join the ranks of the gods and goddesses. These chapters also provide details about specific locations in the underworld as well as the important sacred amulets the dead person should wear for protection.

FASCINATING FACTS ABOUT THE BOOK OF THE DEAD

- The text and headers in the book are written in different colors of ink. The main text is black and the headers are written with red ink.
- The creatures who guard the underworld have very scary titles, like "he who dances using blood."

Did you Know?

Papyrus scroll

- Some of the books prepared for the wealthy were so long that the papyrus scroll used for them was more than 100 feet in length.
- The texts in The Book of the Dead were written over many centuries so the book had many different authors.

- The Papyrus of Ani is a famous version of The Book of the Dead. It's currently housed in London at the British Museum. It was prepared for the scribe Ani and it was written around 1275 BC. It has hieroglyphs written in cursive style and is filled with elaborate illustrations. It was originally a 78-foot scroll of papyrus.

THE PAPYRUS OF ANI

Five shabtis of Herudja, son of Paunhatef

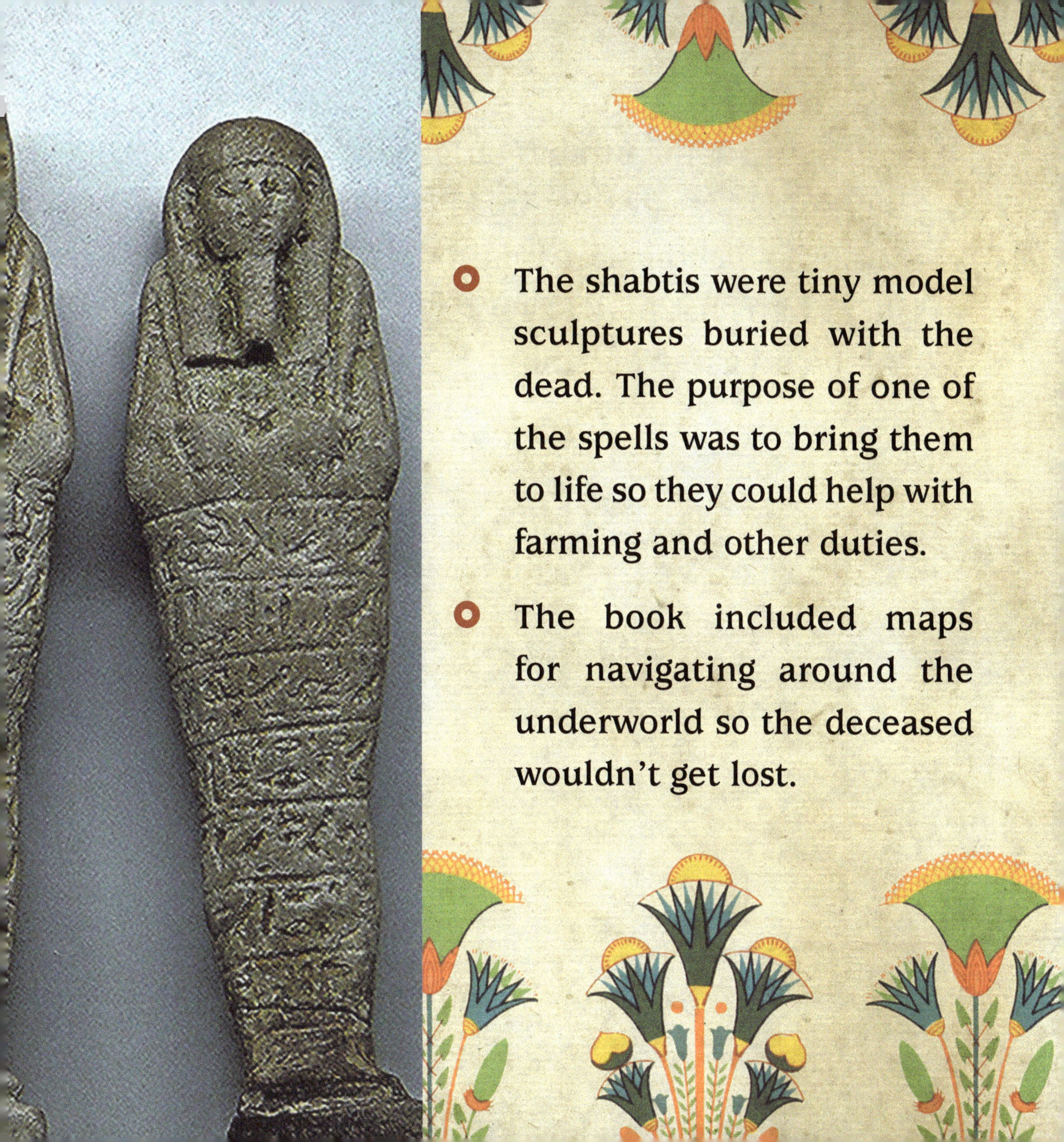

- The shabtis were tiny model sculptures buried with the dead. The purpose of one of the spells was to bring them to life so they could help with farming and other duties.
- The book included maps for navigating around the underworld so the deceased wouldn't get lost.

- Journeys in the underworld were sometimes long and made people tired just like journeys on Earth. So that the deceased could be entertained there were instructions for how to build the board game of Senet.

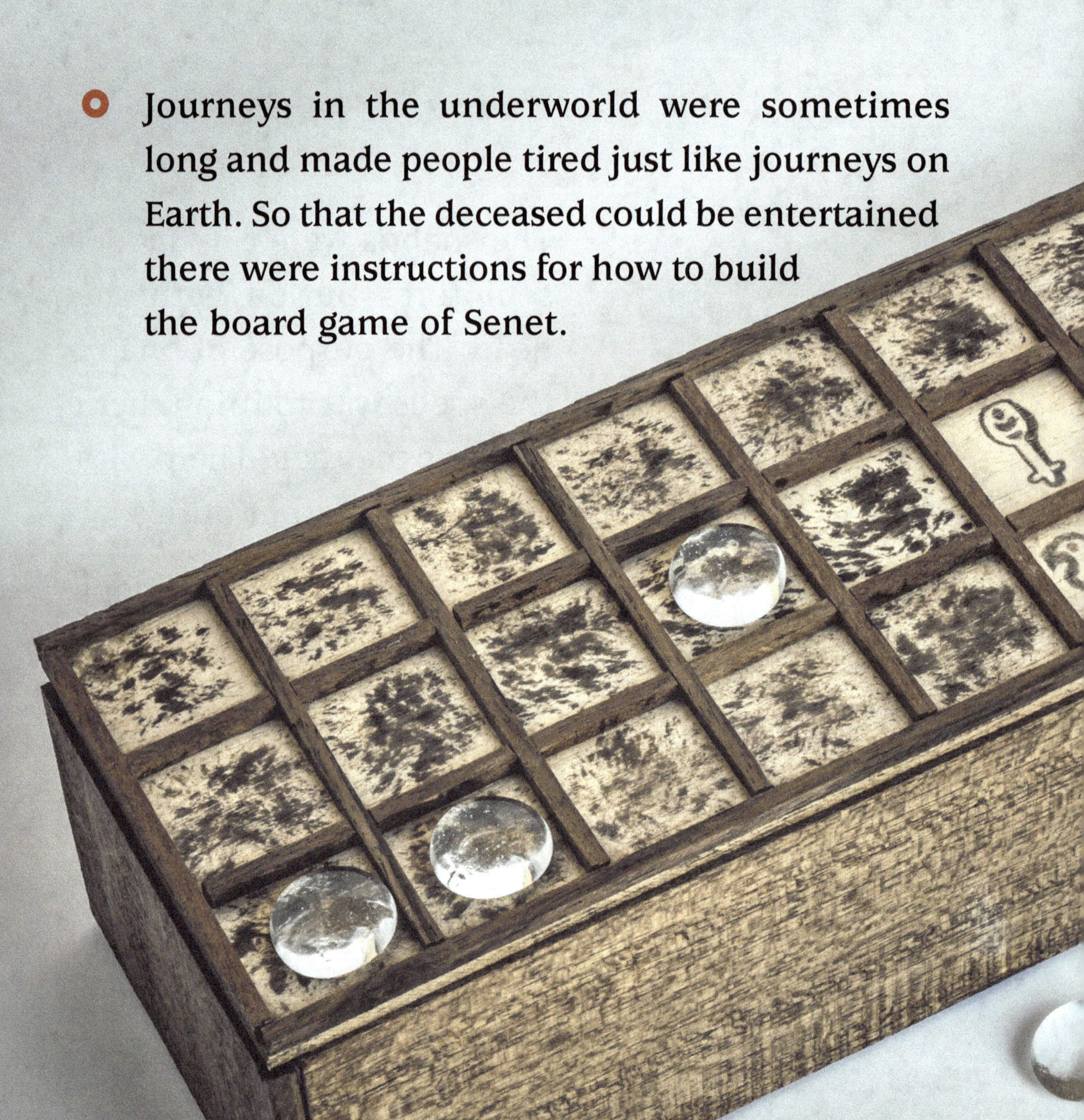

Senet boardgame with dice and pawn

- The Egyptians spent a great deal of their lives on Earth preparing for the day they would die.

- If the deceased person was found worthy, he or she would sail away to heaven in the boat belonging to the important sun god, Ra.

Egyptian sacred barge with tomb floating on the water

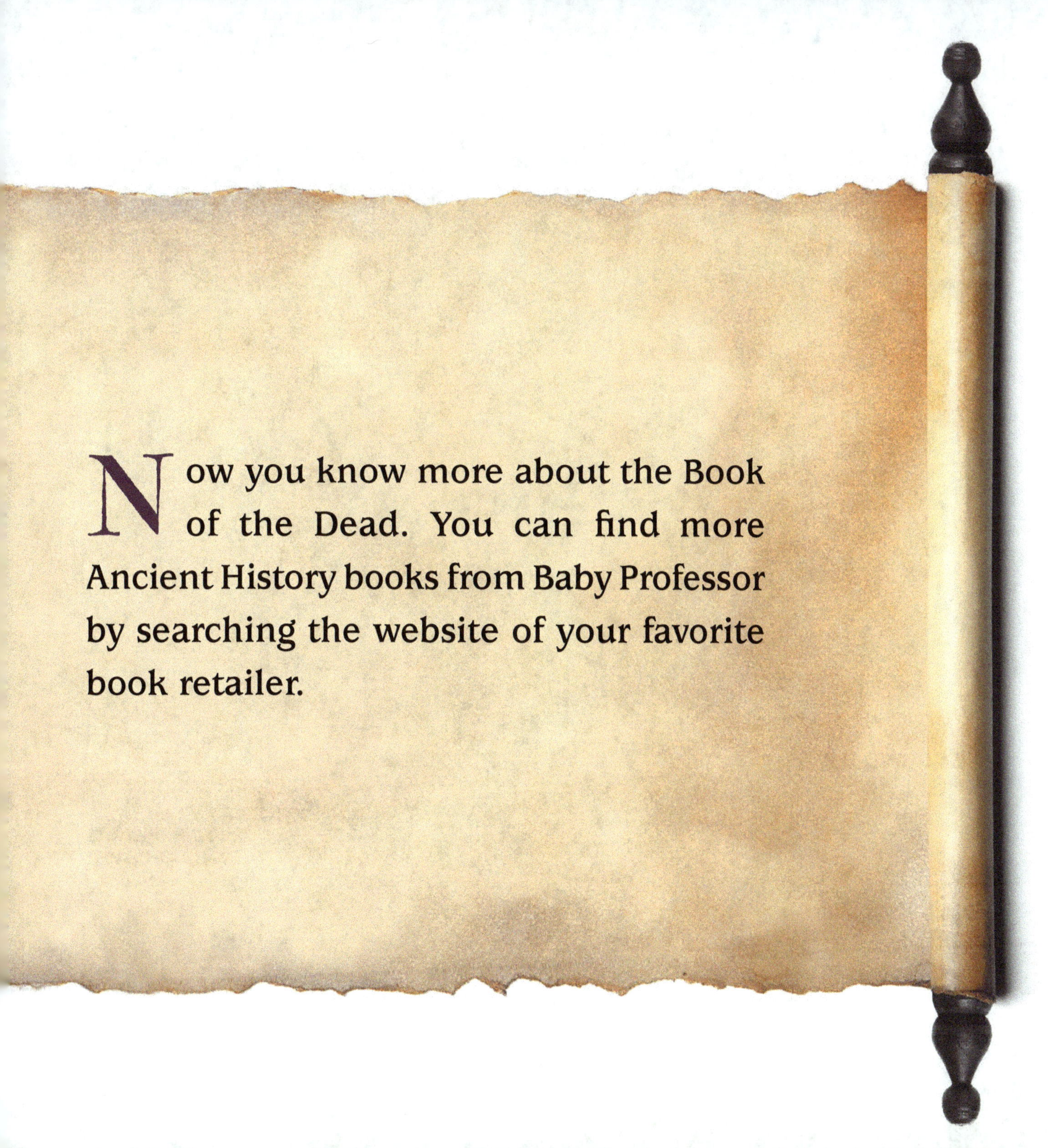

Now you know more about the Book of the Dead. You can find more Ancient History books from Baby Professor by searching the website of your favorite book retailer.

www.ingramcontent.com/pod-product-compliance
Lightning Source LLC
LaVergne TN
LVHW060507170826
845677LV00026B/1638

* 9 7 9 8 8 6 9 4 3 1 1 7 2 *